Table of Contents:

The Advent Calendar: A Time-Honored ....
An explanation of the Advent calendar tradition and how to use this book.

Day 1: Sugar-Dusted Snowflake Cookies Winter's beauty in sugar-dusted treats.

Day 2: Cinnamon Star Cookies (Zimtsterne) Traditional German cinnamon-spiced stars.

Day 3: Cranberry Orange Scones Perfect for a Christmas morning breakfast.

Day 4: Peppermint Mocha Brownies Combining classic coffee and mint flavors.

Day 5: Spiced Nut Brittle A crunchy sweet treat.

Day 6: Gingerbread Latte Cupcakes A delectable fusion of coffee and classic gingerbread spices topped with a creamy frosting.

Day 7: White Chocolate Raspberry Tart Creamy white chocolate ganache with a tart raspberry compote in a buttery crust.

Day 8: Eggnog Crème Brûlée A rich and creamy custard with the flavors of eggnog and a caramelized sugar top.

Day 9: Stollen Bites Miniature versions of the classic German Christmas bread filled with dried fruits and marzipan.

Day 10: Caramel Pecan Pie Bars Buttery shortbread base topped with a gooey caramel and roasted pecan layer.

Day 11: Mulled Wine-Poached Pears Pears poached in a rich mulled wine reduction, perfect for a festive dessert.

Day 12: Chocolate Peppermint Roll Soft chocolate sponge cake rolled with a peppermint whipped cream filling.

Day 13: Fruitcake Cookies All the traditional flavors of a fruitcake condensed into a bite-sized cookie.
Day 14: Mince Pie Pinwheels A modern twist on the classic mince pie, with spiced fruit filling swirled into puff pastry.
Day 15: Coconut Snowballs Luscious coconut truffles, evoke the beauty of fresh winter snow.
Day 16: Spiced Apple Galette Rustic open-faced pie filled with spiced apple slices.
Day 17: Almond Joy Macarons Macarons inspired by the classic candy, with coconut and chocolate ganache filling.
Day 18: Cherry Chocolate Biscotti Twice-baked Italian cookies studded with dried cherries and chocolate chunks.
Day 19: Panettone Muffins Muffin versions of the Italian Christmas bread, dotted with candied fruits and raisins.
Day 20: Glazed Cranberry Orange Loaf Moist loaf cake with tangy cranberries and a sweet orange glaze.
Day 21: Red Velvet Snowflake Cookies Red velvet cookies stamped with snowflake patterns and dusted with powdered sugar.
Day 22: Midnight Chocolate Chestnut Torte A rich chocolate torte with a chestnut puree center, perfect for Christmas Eve indulgence.
Day 23: Tiramisu Trifle Layered dessert with a coffee-soaked sponge, mascarpone cream, and a dusting of cocoa.
Day 24: Traditional Yule Log (Bûche de Noël) symbolizes the grandeur of Christmas Eve. The history and significance of this cake.

The Advent Calendar: A Time-Honored Tradition
The anticipation that builds as December progresses is almost palpable. Snowflakes begin to grace the earth, twinkling lights adorn houses and streets, and there's a certain magic in the air that hints at the festivities to come. Central to many celebrations during this time is the tradition of the Advent calendar.

Originating in the 19th century from German Lutherans, the Advent calendar served as a visual means to count the days leading up to Christmas. Early versions consisted of marking off the days with chalk, while some families lit a new candle for each day. Over time, the tradition evolved, and by the early 20th century, printed calendars with little doors began to appear. Behind each door, a biblical verse, a picture, or, in more recent times, a small treat awaited the eager child who opened it.
This practice of patiently waiting, of unveiling a surprise each day, has become symbolic of the Advent season. It's not just a countdown but a daily ritual of pausing, reflecting, and savoring the journey to Christmas Day.

Celebrating Advent with a Culinary Twist
This Adent journey takes this treasured tradition and infuses it with the warmth and joy of baking. Just as you would open a door on a calendar to discover a small treasure, each day of December in this book reveals a baking recipe for you to explore and enjoy. Think of it as an invitation to embark on a culinary journey, where each step brings new flavors, textures, and techniques into your home.

To get the most out of this book:
1. **Prepare in Advance:** Go through the recipes, make a list of ingredients you'll need, and stock up. This will ensure a smooth baking experience as December rolls around.
2. **Involve Loved Ones:** The magic of Christmas is amplified when shared. Invite family or friends to join you in the kitchen. Let the little ones take charge of simpler tasks. Share the stories, the laughs, and the bakes.
3. **Document the Journey:** Take photos of your creations, jot down notes or modifications you made, and record your thoughts and memories. Over the years, this will transform your book into a cherished keepsake.
4. **Gift Your Creations:** If you find yourself with an abundance of treats, consider gifting some to neighbors, friends, or local community centers. After all, the spirit of Christmas is in giving.
5. **Reflect and Enjoy:** While the recipes and bakes are the stars, take a moment each day to reflect on the meaning of the season, the joy of the process, and the love that surrounds you.

This book is more than just a collection of recipes—it's a celebration of the days leading up to Christmas, a reminder of the simple joys of life, and a nudge to indulge in the delights of the festive season. So, don your apron, preheat the oven, and let's make this Advent a deliciously memorable one!

Day 1: Sugar-Dusted Snowflake Cookies

Description and Significance:
Snowflakes, each uniquely intricate and delicate, are one of nature's most beautiful symbols of winter. Just as every snowflake has its unique pattern, each family has its special holiday traditions.

These Sugar-Dusted Snowflake Cookies capture the ethereal beauty of snowflakes, bringing a touch of winter wonderland into your home. As the first treat in our Advent Calendar, they set the tone for the festive season, reminding us of the magic of winter and the joy of sharing with loved ones!

Sugar-Dusted Snowflake Cookies Recipe:
Ingredients:
- 2 1/2 cups all-purpose flour
- 1/4 teaspoon baking powder
- 1/4 teaspoon salt
- 1 cup unsalted butter, softened
- 1 cup granulated sugar
- 1 large egg
- 1 teaspoon pure vanilla extract
- Powdered sugar, for dusting

Instructions:
1. **Prepare the Dry Ingredients:** In a medium-sized bowl, whisk together the flour, baking powder, and salt. Set aside.
2. **Cream Butter and Sugar:** In a large bowl, using an electric mixer, beat the softened butter and granulated sugar on medium speed until the mixture is smooth and creamy, typically about 3-5 minutes.
3. **Add Egg and Vanilla:** Beat in the egg and vanilla extract until fully combined.
4. **Gradually Mix in Dry Ingredients:** Reduce the mixer's speed to low and slowly add the dry ingredient mixture, blending just until the dough comes together.
5. **Chill the Dough:** Divide the dough in half and flatten each portion into a disk. Wrap each disk tightly in plastic wrap and refrigerate for at least 2 hours, or overnight.
6. **Preheat the Oven:** Position a rack in the middle of your oven and preheat it to 350°F (175°C). Line two baking sheets with parchment paper.

7. **Roll and Cut:** On a lightly floured surface, roll out one disk of the chilled dough to a thickness of about 1/8 inch. Using a snowflake-shaped cookie cutter, cut out the cookies and place them on the prepared baking sheets, ensuring there's space between each cookie.
8. **Bake:** Place the cookies in the preheated oven and bake for 10-12 minutes, or until the edges are lightly golden. Be sure to rotate the baking sheets halfway through the baking time for even baking.
9. **Cool:** Remove the cookies from the oven and allow them to cool on the baking sheets for 5 minutes. Afterward, transfer them to a wire rack to cool completely.
10. **Dust:** Once the cookies are completely cooled, sprinkle generously with powdered sugar using a fine sieve or a sugar shaker.

Serving Suggestion: These snowflake cookies pair wonderfully with a cup of hot cocoa or mulled wine. The delicate dusting of sugar mimics the fresh snowfall, making them a delightful treat for cozy winter evenings.

Note: You can also use this recipe as a base for other shapes and decorations, but the simplicity of the powdered sugar on the snowflake shape truly embodies the serene beauty of winter.

Day 2: Cinnamon Star Cookies (Zimtsterne)

Description and Significance:

The Cinnamon Star, or Zimtsterne in German, is a quintessential Christmas cookie hailing from Germany. Traditionally enjoyed during the Advent season, these almond-based treats are wonderfully aromatic, with a rich cinnamon scent that fills the kitchen as they bake. The star shape, symbolic of the Star of Bethlehem, is reminiscent of the Christmas story, making these cookies both a delightful treat and a meaningful reminder of the season's deeper significance.

Cinnamon Star Cookies (Zimtsterne) Recipe:
Ingredients:
- 3 cups almond flour or finely ground almonds
- 1 1/2 cups powdered sugar, plus extra for dusting
- 2 teaspoons ground cinnamon
- 3 large egg whites
- 1/4 teaspoon cream of tartar
- 1 teaspoon pure vanilla extract
- Zest of 1 lemon

Instructions:
1. **Prepare the Almond Mixture:** In a large mixing bowl, combine the almond flour, 1 cup of powdered sugar, and ground cinnamon. Stir until well mixed.
2. **Whip Egg Whites:** In a separate, clean bowl, beat the egg whites and cream of tartar until soft peaks form. Gradually add the remaining 1/2 cup of powdered sugar and continue beating until you have stiff, glossy peaks.
3. **Combine Mixtures:** Reserve about 1/2 cup of the whipped egg whites for the topping. Slowly fold the remaining egg whites into the almond mixture, adding the vanilla extract and lemon zest. The dough should be sticky but manageable.
4. **Chill:** Wrap the dough in plastic wrap and refrigerate for at least 1 hour.
5. **Preheat Oven:** Position a rack in the center of the oven and preheat it to 325°F (163°C). Line two baking sheets with parchment paper.
6. **Roll and Shape:** On a surface lightly dusted with powdered sugar, roll out the dough to about 1/4 inch thickness. Using a star-shaped cookie cutter, cut out the cookies and place them on the prepared baking sheets.

7. **Top with Reserved Egg Whites:** Gently brush the top of each cookie with the reserved egg white mixture. This will give the cookies a nice, shiny finish after baking.
8. **Bake:** Bake the cookies in the preheated oven for about 12-15 minutes, or until the edges are lightly golden and the tops have set.
9. **Cool:** Allow the cookies to cool on the baking sheets for about 5 minutes, then transfer to a wire rack to cool completely.

Serving Suggestion: Embark on this European adventure, savoring each bite of history and tradition with these Cinnamon Star Cookies!

Zimtsterne are particularly delightful when paired with a hot cup of tea or mulled wine. The spicy aroma of cinnamon coupled with the nutty undertones of almonds make for a cookie that's rich in flavors and steeped in tradition.

Note: While the cookies are delicious when freshly baked, they also age well. Store them in an airtight container, and over a few days, they'll become even more tender and flavorful.

Day 3: Cranberry Orange Scones

Description and Significance:
Amid the festive hustle and bustle, there's something uniquely comforting about a tranquil Christmas morning breakfast. Cranberry Orange Scones are a perfect centerpiece for such a setting.

The tartness of the cranberries melds with the sweet citrus notes of orange, creating a delightful symphony of flavors. Each bite encapsulates the brightness of a winter morning and the warmth of holiday traditions. Symbolically, cranberries with their vibrant red hue remind us of the joy and vitality of the season, while oranges, often found in Christmas stockings, evoke nostalgia and sentiment.

Cranberry Orange Scones Recipe:
Ingredients:
- 2 1/2 cups all-purpose flour
- 1/4 cup granulated sugar, plus 1 tablespoon for sprinkling
- 1 tablespoon baking powder
- 1/2 teaspoon salt
- 1/2 cup unsalted butter, chilled and cubed
- 2/3 cup whole milk
- 1 large egg
- Zest of 2 oranges
- 1 tablespoon orange juice
- 1 cup fresh cranberries, chopped
- Optional: 1/2 cup white chocolate chips

Instructions:
1. **Dry Ingredients:** In a large bowl, whisk together the flour, 1/4 cup of granulated sugar, baking powder, and salt.
2. **Butter Incorporation:** Using a pastry cutter or two knives, cut the chilled butter into the flour mixture until it resembles coarse crumbs.
3. **Wet Ingredients:** In a separate bowl, whisk together the milk, egg, orange zest, and orange juice. Slowly pour this into the dry mixture, stirring until just combined.
4. **Add Cranberries:** Gently fold in the chopped cranberries (and white chocolate chips if using) until they are evenly distributed throughout the dough.
5. **Preheat the Oven:** Position a rack in the center of the oven and preheat to 400°F (200°C). Line a baking sheet with parchment paper.

6. **Shape Scones:** On a lightly floured surface, knead the dough a few times, then shape it into a circle, about 1 inch thick. Using a sharp knife, cut the circle into 8 equal wedges.
7. **Transfer and Sprinkle:** Place the scone wedges on the prepared baking sheet, spaced apart. Sprinkle the tops with the remaining tablespoon of granulated sugar.
8. **Bake:** Place the scones in the oven and bake for 15-18 minutes, or until they are golden brown on top and a toothpick inserted into the center comes out clean.
9. **Cool:** Allow the scones to cool on the baking sheet for 5 minutes, then transfer them to a wire rack to cool slightly before serving.

Serving Suggestion: Awaken your senses and embrace the festivity of the season with these cranberry-orange scones, perfect for a serene Christmas morning!

These scones are a match made in heaven with clotted cream and marmalade. The creamy texture complements the crumbly scone, and the sweet marmalade enhances the tangy flavors of cranberry and orange.

Note: Scones are best enjoyed fresh. However, if you want to prep ahead, you can freeze the unbaked scone wedges and bake them on Christmas morning, adding a few extra minutes to the baking time.

Day 4: Peppermint Mocha Brownies

Description and Significance:
Few flavors capture the essence of the festive season quite like peppermint mocha. It's a classic combination that evokes memories of brisk winter walks and cozy afternoons by the fire. By integrating these flavors into a rich and chewy brownie, we offer a sophisticated take on the traditional festive treat. The strong coffee notes and refreshing peppermint come together harmoniously, making each bite a delightful contrast of warm and cool sensations.

Peppermint Mocha Brownies Recipe:
Ingredients:
- 1/2 cup unsalted butter
- 8 ounces semi-sweet chocolate, coarsely chopped
- 1 cup granulated sugar
- 3 large eggs
- 1 teaspoon pure vanilla extract
- 1 tablespoon instant espresso powder (or strong instant coffee)
- 3/4 cup all-purpose flour
- 1/4 cup unsweetened cocoa powder
- 1/2 teaspoon salt
- 1/2 cup peppermint candies or candy canes, crushed
- Optional: 1/4 teaspoon peppermint extract for an extra minty kick

Instructions:
1. **Melt Butter and Chocolate:** In a medium saucepan over low heat, melt the butter and chocolate together, stirring continuously until smooth and combined. Remove from heat and allow it to cool slightly.
2. **Preheat the Oven:** Position a rack in the center of the oven and preheat to 350°F (175°C). Line an 8x8-inch baking pan with parchment paper, leaving an overhang on two opposite sides (this will help in lifting the brownies out later).
3. **Mix Sugar and Wet Ingredients:** To the melted chocolate mixture, add the sugar, mixing well. Beat in the eggs one at a time, ensuring each is fully incorporated. Stir in the vanilla extract and, if using, the peppermint extract.

4. **Incorporate Coffee:** Dissolve the espresso powder in a tablespoon of hot water and add it to the mixture, blending well.
5. **Add Dry Ingredients:** Sift the flour, cocoa powder, and salt into the wet mixture. Fold gently, ensuring not to overmix.
6. **Transfer and Top:** Pour the batter into the prepared baking pan and smooth the top using a spatula. Sprinkle the crushed peppermint candies or candy canes evenly over the top.
7. **Bake:** Place in the oven and bake for about 25-30 minutes, or until a toothpick inserted into the center comes out with a few moist crumbs.
8. **Cool and Cut:** Allow the brownies to cool completely in the pan set on a wire rack. Once cooled, use the parchment paper overhangs to lift out the brownies and place them on a cutting board. Using a sharp knife, cut into squares.

Serving Suggestion: Indulge in the magic of the holiday season with these Peppermint Mocha Brownies, a treat that masterfully interweaves the classic flavors of coffee and mint!

These brownies are perfect alongside a cup of steaming hot cocoa or a latte. The rich coffee and chocolate flavors combined with the cool peppermint create a sensory delight that's truly emblematic of the festive season.

Note: For those who are fervent mint lovers, adding the optional peppermint extract gives that extra minty kick, amplifying the seasonal feel of the brownies.

Day 5: Spiced Nut Brittle

Description and Significance:
Nut brittle has been a beloved treat for generations, with its origins tracing back to ancient civilizations. This Spiced Nut Brittle gives a festive twist to the classic, incorporating warm spices reminiscent of the winter season. The crackling texture combined with aromatic spices and toasted nuts conjures images of glowing hearths and festive gatherings, making it a delightful treat to share during the holidays.

Spiced Nut Brittle Recipe:
Ingredients:
- 1 cup granulated sugar
- 1/2 cup light corn syrup
- 1/4 teaspoon salt
- 1/4 cup water
- 1 cup mixed nuts (like almonds, pecans, walnuts, and cashews), toasted
- 1 teaspoon vanilla extract
- 1/4 teaspoon baking soda
- 1/2 teaspoon ground cinnamon
- 1/4 teaspoon ground nutmeg
- 1/4 teaspoon ground cloves
- 1/4 teaspoon ground allspice
- 2 tablespoons unsalted butter, softened
- Optional: a pinch of cayenne pepper for a spicy kick

Instructions:
1. **Prep Work:** Grease a large baking sheet or line it with a silicone baking mat. Have all ingredients measured out and ready, as the process can be fast-paced once started.
2. **Combine Sugars and Liquids:** In a heavy-bottomed saucepan, combine the sugar, corn syrup, salt, and water. Cook over medium heat, stirring constantly until the sugar dissolves.
3. **Boil Without Stirring:** Increase the heat to medium-high and bring the mixture to a boil. Continue boiling without stirring, but keep an eye on it to prevent it from burning.
4. **Check Temperature:** Using a candy thermometer, monitor the mixture until it reaches 300°F (150°C) – the hard-crack stage.

5. **Add Remaining Ingredients:** Once the desired temperature is reached, remove the saucepan from heat. Quickly stir in the toasted nuts, butter, vanilla extract, baking soda, and spices (including the optional cayenne pepper if desired). Mix well.
6. **Spread on Baking Sheet:** Pour the brittle mixture onto the prepared baking sheet, spreading it thinly with a spatula. Try to spread the nuts out evenly.
7. **Cool and Break:** Allow the brittle to cool completely at room temperature. This may take an hour or more. Once it's set, break the brittle into shards or bite-sized pieces using your hands or the back of a spoon.

Serving Suggestion: Dive into a crunchy symphony of flavors and textures with this Spiced Nut Brittle, perfectly capturing the warmth and generosity of the festive season!

Spiced Nut Brittle makes a wonderful gift when packaged in cellophane bags tied with festive ribbons. It's also a delightful accompaniment to coffee or spiced tea, offering a sweet and spicy crunch with every sip.

Note: Be extremely cautious when working with the sugar syrup, as it gets scalding hot. Make sure to keep kids and pets at a safe distance during the process.

Day 6: Gingerbread Latte Cupcakes

Description and Significance:
The magic of the holiday season often comes alive with the enticing aroma of gingerbread wafting through the home. Combine this with the comforting notes of coffee, and you have the Gingerbread Latte Cupcake!

It encapsulates the essence of a cozy winter afternoon. With a perfect balance of spicy gingerbread and rich coffee, each cupcake is a delightful nod to those cherished moments shared over a steaming mug during the festive season.

Gingerbread Latte Cupcakes Recipe:
Ingredients:
For the Cupcakes:
- 1 1/2 cups all-purpose flour
- 1 teaspoon baking powder
- 1/2 teaspoon baking soda
- 2 teaspoons ground ginger
- 1 teaspoon ground cinnamon
- 1/4 teaspoon ground cloves
- 1/4 teaspoon ground nutmeg
- 1/2 cup unsalted butter, softened
- 1/2 cup dark brown sugar, packed
- 2 large eggs
- 1/2 cup molasses
- 1/2 cup brewed strong coffee, cooled
- 1/4 cup milk

For the Creamy Frosting:
- 1/2 cup unsalted butter, softened
- 3 cups powdered sugar
- 3 tablespoons brewed coffee, cooled
- 1 teaspoon vanilla extract
- Optional: Crushed gingerbread cookies or sprinkles for topping

Instructions:
1. **Preheat the Oven:** Position a rack in the middle of the oven and preheat to 350°F (175°C). Line a 12-cup muffin tin with paper liners.
2. **Dry Ingredients:** In a medium bowl, whisk together the flour, baking powder, baking soda, ginger, cinnamon, cloves, and nutmeg. Set aside.
3. **Cream Butter and Sugar:** In a large bowl, cream together the butter and dark brown sugar until light

and fluffy. Beat in the eggs one at a time, then stir in the molasses.
4. **Alternate Wet and Dry Mixes:** Gradually blend the dry ingredient mixture into the creamed mixture, alternating with the coffee and milk. Begin and end with the dry ingredients. Mix until just combined.
5. **Fill Cupcake Liners:** Pour the batter into the prepared muffin tin, filling each liner about 2/3 full.
6. **Bake:** Place the tin in the oven and bake for 18-20 minutes, or until a toothpick inserted into the center of a cupcake comes out clean.
7. **Cool:** Remove from the oven and allow the cupcakes to cool in the tin for 5 minutes. Transfer to a wire rack and let them cool completely.

For the Frosting:
1. **Beat Butter:** In a large mixing bowl, beat the butter until smooth and creamy.
2. **Add Ingredients Gradually:** Slowly add in the powdered sugar, coffee, and vanilla extract. Beat until the frosting is smooth and spreadable. If the frosting is too thick, you can add a splash of more coffee or milk to thin it out.
3. **Frost Cupcakes:** Once the cupcakes are completely cooled, frost each one generously with the creamy coffee frosting.
4. **Decorate:** If desired, top the frosted cupcakes with crushed gingerbread cookies or festive sprinkles for an added touch.

Serving Suggestion: Immerse yourself in the delightful fusion of coffee and gingerbread spices, and let the Gingerbread Latte Cupcakes transport you to a cozy winter wonderland, replete with the joys of the festive season.

Serve the cupcakes alongside a steaming mug of coffee or hot cocoa for a delightful afternoon treat.

Day 7: White Chocolate Raspberry Tart

Description and Significance:
The White Chocolate Raspberry Tart is a testament to the art of harmonizing contrasts. The luxurious sweetness of white chocolate coupled with the tartness of raspberries creates a symphony of flavors, each complementing the other.

This tart, with its buttery crust, cradling a luscious filling, is reminiscent of snow-covered berry bushes on a frosty winter morning – a true celebration of the season's beauty and bounty!

White Chocolate Raspberry Tart Recipe:
Ingredients:
For the Buttery Crust:
- 1 1/4 cups all-purpose flour
- 1/4 cup granulated sugar
- 1/2 cup unsalted butter, cold and cubed
- 1 large egg yolk
- 1-2 tablespoons cold water

For the Raspberry Compote:
- 2 cups fresh or frozen raspberries
- 1/4 cup granulated sugar
- 1 tablespoon lemon juice
- 1 tablespoon cornstarch

For the White Chocolate Ganache:
- 8 oz. white chocolate, finely chopped
- 1/2 cup heavy cream

Instructions:
1. **Prepare the Crust:** In a food processor, pulse together the flour and sugar. Add the cold butter and pulse until the mixture resembles coarse crumbs. Add the egg yolk and 1 tablespoon of cold water. Pulse until the dough begins to come together. If needed, add an additional tablespoon of water. Press the dough into a disc, wrap it in plastic wrap, and refrigerate for at least 30 minutes.
2. **Preheat Oven:** Preheat your oven to 375°F (190°C).
3. **Roll and Bake the Crust:** On a floured surface, roll out the dough to fit a 9-inch tart pan. Press the dough into the pan and trim any excess. Prick the base with a fork and bake for 15-20 minutes or until lightly golden. Remove from the oven and let cool.

4. **Prepare the Raspberry Compote:** In a saucepan, combine raspberries, sugar, and lemon juice. Cook over medium heat, mashing the raspberries slightly until they release their juices. In a small bowl, mix the cornstarch with 2 tablespoons of cold water to create a slurry, then add it to the raspberries. Cook for another 2-3 minutes or until thickened. Remove from heat and allow it to cool.
5. **Make the White Chocolate Ganache:** In a saucepan, heat the heavy cream until it's just beginning to simmer. Place the finely chopped white chocolate in a bowl, and pour the hot cream over it. Let it sit for a minute, then stir until smooth and well combined.
6. **Assemble the Tart:** Spread the raspberry compote over the cooled tart crust. Pour the white chocolate ganache over the raspberry layer, spreading it evenly.
7. **Chill:** Place the tart in the refrigerator and allow it to set for at least 2 hours.
8. **Serve:** Before serving, you can garnish with fresh raspberries or a dusting of powdered sugar if desired.

Serving Suggestion: With every bite of the White Chocolate Raspberry Tart, journey through layers of delight – from the crisp, buttery crust to the tangy compote and the velvety ganache, each element is a holiday treat for the senses.

This tart pairs beautifully with a dollop of whipped cream or a scoop of vanilla ice cream.

Day 8: Eggnog Crème Brûlée

Description and Significance:
Crème Brûlée, a dessert adored for its elegance and contrasting textures, becomes even more enchanting when given a holiday twist with the flavors of eggnog. A concoction of creamy custard beneath a crackling caramel crown, this Eggnog Crème Brûlée pays homage to both the beloved French dessert and the traditional festive beverage. It's the perfect embodiment of Christmas cheer, offering warmth, sweetness, and a touch of spice in every spoonful.

Eggnog Crème Brûlée Recipe:
Ingredients:
For the Eggnog Custard:
- 2 cups heavy cream
- 1/2 cup granulated sugar, divided
- 5 large egg yolks
- 1 teaspoon pure vanilla extract
- 1/2 teaspoon ground nutmeg
- 1/4 teaspoon ground cinnamon
- 1/4 cup dark rum or brandy (optional)

For the Caramelized Sugar Top:
- 4-6 tablespoons granulated sugar

Instructions:
1. **Preheat the Oven:** Position a rack in the center of the oven and preheat to 325°F (160°C).
2. **Heat the Cream:** In a medium saucepan, heat the heavy cream, half of the sugar (1/4 cup), nutmeg, and cinnamon over medium heat, stirring occasionally, until the mixture is hot but not boiling.
3. **Whisk Egg Yolks:** In a separate bowl, whisk together the egg yolks and the remaining 1/4 cup of sugar until well combined.
4. **Temper the Egg Mixture:** Slowly pour a small amount of the hot cream mixture into the egg yolk mixture, whisking constantly to prevent the eggs from scrambling. Continue to slowly add the rest of the hot cream, whisking continuously.
5. **Add Flavorings:** Stir in the vanilla extract and, if using, the dark rum or brandy.
6. **Prepare Ramekins:** Pour the mixture through a fine-mesh sieve into a large measuring cup or bowl with a pour spout. Then, divide the custard mixture evenly among four 6-ounce ramekins.

7. **Bain-Marie:** Place the ramekins in a large baking dish. Pour enough hot water into the baking dish to come halfway up the sides of the ramekins. This water bath helps cook the custards gently and evenly.
8. **Bake:** Transfer the baking dish to the oven and bake for 40-45 minutes, or until the centers of the custards are just set but still slightly wobbly.
9. **Cool:** Remove the ramekins from the water bath and let them cool to room temperature. Once cooled, cover them with plastic wrap and refrigerate for at least 4 hours, or preferably overnight.
10. **Caramelize the Sugar:** Before serving, sprinkle about 1 to 1.5 tablespoons of granulated sugar evenly over the surface of each custard. Using a kitchen torch, caramelize the sugar until it's golden and bubbly. Alternatively, you can place the ramekins under a preheated broiler for 1-2 minutes, watching closely, until the sugar is caramelized.

Serving Suggestion: This Eggnog Crème Brûlée is more than just a dessert; it's a decadent experience, evoking nostalgic memories of Christmases past while creating new, delightful ones.

Allow the crème brûlée to sit for a few minutes to let the caramelized sugar harden, creating that signature crackling top. Serve immediately and enjoy the magical blend of creaminess, crunch, and festive flavors.

Day 9: Stollen Bites

Description and Significance:
Stollen, a traditional German Christmas bread, finds a delightful twist in these bite-sized treats. Each bite delivers the same richness and festive flavors as its larger counterpart but in a form that's perfect for snacking and sharing.

Studded with dried fruits and a hidden marzipan center, these Stollen Bites seamlessly merge centuries-old traditions with modern festivity, ensuring every holiday gathering is filled with a touch of old-world charm.

Stollen Bites Recipe:
Ingredients:
For the Dough:
- 2 1/2 cups all-purpose flour
- 1/4 cup granulated sugar
- 1 packet (2 1/4 teaspoons) active dry yeast
- 1/2 cup warm milk (110°F or 45°C)
- 1/4 cup unsalted butter, softened
- 1 large egg
- 1/2 teaspoon salt
- 1 teaspoon ground cardamom
- 1/2 teaspoon ground nutmeg

For the Filling:
- 1/2 cup mixed dried fruits (such as raisins, currants, and chopped dried apricots)
- 1/4 cup rum or orange juice
- 1/2 cup marzipan, divided into small balls
- 1/2 teaspoon almond extract
- Zest of 1 lemon

For the Topping:
- Melted butter, for brushing
- Powdered sugar, for dusting

Instructions:
1. **Prepare the Dried Fruits:** In a small bowl, combine the mixed dried fruits and rum (or orange juice). Let them soak for at least an hour, preferably overnight.
2. **Activate the Yeast:** In a separate bowl, combine the warm milk and sugar. Sprinkle the yeast on top and let it sit for 5-10 minutes, or until frothy.
3. **Mix the Dough:** In a large mixing bowl, combine the flour, softened butter, egg, salt, cardamom, and

nutmeg. Pour in the yeast mixture and mix until a soft dough forms.
4. **Knead:** Turn the dough onto a floured surface and knead for about 8-10 minutes, or until smooth and elastic.
5. **First Rise:** Place the dough in a greased bowl, covering it with a damp cloth. Allow it to rise in a warm place for about 1 hour, or until it has doubled in size.
6. **Add Fruits and Marzipan:** Punch down the dough and flatten it out on a floured surface. Sprinkle the soaked dried fruits, almond extract, and lemon zest over the dough, folding and kneading until they're evenly distributed. Divide the dough into small portions. Flatten each portion, place a marzipan ball in the center, and seal the dough around it, shaping it into balls.
7. **Second Rise:** Place the Stollen Bites on a baking sheet lined with parchment paper, leaving space between each one. Cover them with a cloth and let them rise for another 30-40 minutes.
8. **Preheat Oven:** While the bites are rising, preheat your oven to 375°F (190°C).
9. **Bake:** Uncover the stollen bites and bake for 15-20 minutes, or until they are golden brown.
10. **Finish the Bites:** Once out of the oven, while still warm, brush each Stollen Bite with melted butter and generously dust with powdered sugar.

Serving Suggestion: Capturing the heart of German Christmas traditions, these Stollen Bites offer a tantalizing blend of flavors and textures, making them a must-have for every holiday spread. Whether gifted in a festive tin or served on a platter, they're bound to spread joy and nostalgia in every bite.

Serve these bites with a cup of hot cocoa or mulled wine for a truly festive experience.

Day 10: Caramel Pecan Pie Bars

Description and Significance:
With the heartwarming allure of classic pecan pie and the convenience of handheld treats, Caramel Pecan Pie Bars are a testament to the union of tradition and modernity. A buttery shortbread forms the foundation, cradling a layer of sumptuous caramel and toasted pecans.

These bars capture the essence of festive gatherings and cozy moments! Much like the time you spend with your family during Advent, Pecan Pie Bars are an irreplaceably nutty and sweet part of holiday indulgences!

Caramel Pecan Pie Bars Recipe:
Ingredients:
For the Shortbread Base:
- 1 cup unsalted butter, softened
- 1/2 cup granulated sugar
- 2 cups all-purpose flour
- 1/4 teaspoon salt

For the Caramel Pecan Topping:
- 1 cup unsalted butter
- 1 cup light brown sugar, packed
- 1/4 cup honey
- 2 tablespoons heavy cream
- 2 cups pecan halves, toasted
- 1 teaspoon vanilla extract
- 1/4 teaspoon salt

Instructions:
1. **Preheat Oven:** Preheat the oven to 350°F (175°C). Line a 9x13-inch baking pan with parchment paper, allowing some overhang for easy removal.
2. **Prepare the Shortbread Base:** In a mixing bowl, cream together the softened butter and granulated sugar until light and fluffy. Gradually add in the flour and salt, mixing until the dough comes together. Press the dough evenly into the bottom of the prepared baking pan. Bake for 15-18 minutes or until the edges are lightly golden.
3. **Make the Caramel Pecan Topping:** In a heavy-bottomed saucepan, combine the butter, brown sugar, honey, and heavy cream. Bring the mixture to a boil over medium heat, stirring constantly. Once boiling, continue to cook for 1 minute without stirring. Remove from heat and stir in the toasted pecans, vanilla extract, and salt.

4. **Add Topping to Base:** Pour the caramel pecan mixture over the baked shortbread base, spreading it out evenly.
5. **Bake Again:** Return the pan to the oven and bake for an additional 20-25 minutes, or until the caramel layer is bubbly and has a deep golden color.
6. **Cool and Cut:** Allow the bars to cool completely in the pan set on a wire rack. Once cooled, use the parchment overhangs to lift out the slab. Place it on a cutting board and, using a sharp knife, cut it into bars or squares.

Serving Suggestion: The Caramel Pecan Pie Bars seamlessly integrate the elegance of a classic pie with the ease of a bar, offering a delightful crunch from the pecans and a silky sweetness from the caramel. Whether it's for a holiday potluck, a gift for a loved one, or a treat for oneself, these bars embody the comforting essence of the festive season in every bite.

These bars are rich and indulgent, making them perfect with a cup of black coffee or a glass of cold milk. For an added treat, serve them with a dollop of whipped cream or a scoop of vanilla ice cream.

Day 11: Mulled Wine-Poached Pears

Description and Significance:
Mulled Wine-Poached Pears capture the very essence of winter wonderment, invoking memories of crackling fires, starry nights, and jovial gatherings. The deep crimson of the wine, interlaced with spices like clove and star anise, transforms the humble pear into a luxurious, aromatic dessert. This dish brings together the robustness of mulled wine with the delicate nature of pears, creating a symphony of flavors that celebrate the season's best.

Mulled Wine-Poached Pears Recipe:
Ingredients:
- 4 ripe but firm Bosc or Anjou pears, peeled with stems intact
- 1 bottle (750ml) red wine (a medium-bodied wine like Merlot or Cabernet Sauvignon works best)
- 1 cup granulated sugar
- 1 orange, zested and juiced
- 1 lemon, zested and juiced
- 2 cinnamon sticks
- 6 whole cloves
- 3-star anise
- 1 vanilla bean, split lengthwise, or 1 teaspoon vanilla extract
- Optional: Whipped cream or vanilla ice cream, for serving

Instructions:
1. **Prepare the Pears:** Peel the pears, ensuring to keep their stems intact. Slice a thin layer off the bottom of each pear to help them stand upright.
2. **Mix the Poaching Liquid:** In a large pot, combine the wine, sugar, orange zest, orange juice, lemon zest, lemon juice, cinnamon sticks, cloves, star anise, and vanilla bean (or extract). Stir everything together over medium heat until the sugar dissolves.
3. **Poach the Pears:** Once the sugar is dissolved and the mixture is heated, gently place the pears into the pot, ensuring they are fully submerged in the wine mixture. If they're not, add a bit more wine or water until they are.
4. **Gentle Simmer:** Bring the mixture to a low boil, then reduce the heat to maintain a gentle simmer.

Let the pears poach for 25-30 minutes, turning occasionally for even color, or until they are tender but not mushy.

5. **Cool and Steep:** Remove the pot from heat and let the pears cool in the liquid. For deeper flavor, you can refrigerate them in the poaching liquid overnight.
6. **Reduce the Poaching Liquid:** If serving immediately, remove the pears from the pot. Bring the poaching liquid back to a boil and reduce it by half or until it thickens into a syrupy consistency. This usually takes about 15-20 minutes.
7. **Serve:** To serve, place each pear on a dessert plate and drizzle with the reduced wine syrup. Add a dollop of whipped cream or a scoop of vanilla ice cream for added indulgence.

Serving Suggestion: Mulled Wine-Poached Pears are a celebration of winter's flavors. The warming spices and the richness of wine make it an ideal dessert for festive dinners, offering a harmonious blend of simplicity and sophistication that never fails to impress.

Consider garnishing the plate with some orange zest or grated dark chocolate for an extra touch of elegance. This dessert pairs wonderfully with a glass of the same wine used for poaching or a warm cup of spiced tea.

Day 12: Chocolate Peppermint Roll

Description and Significance:
The Chocolate Peppermint Roll marries the bittersweet depth of cocoa with the invigorating freshness of peppermint in a swirl of holiday delight. This dessert, reminiscent of a yule log, harks back to ancient winter solstice traditions, embodying the spirit of warmth and renewal in the heart of the cold season. The softness of the sponge cake combined with the creamy filling creates a dessert as visually enchanting as it is delectably indulgent.

Chocolate Peppermint Roll Recipe:
Ingredients:
For the Chocolate Sponge Cake:
- 4 large eggs, separated
- 1/2 cup granulated sugar
- 1 teaspoon vanilla extract
- 1/2 cup all-purpose flour
- 1/4 cup unsweetened cocoa powder
- 1/4 teaspoon salt
- 1/2 teaspoon cream of tartar

For the Peppermint Whipped Cream Filling:
- 2 cups heavy whipping cream
- 1/2 cup powdered sugar
- 1 teaspoon peppermint extract
- Crushed candy canes or peppermint candies for garnish

Instructions:
1. **Preheat Oven:** Preheat your oven to 350°F (175°C). Line a 15x10-inch jelly roll pan with parchment paper and lightly grease.
2. **Make the Sponge Cake:** In a large bowl, beat the egg yolks with half of the granulated sugar until thick and pale. Mix in vanilla extract. Sift together the flour, cocoa powder, and salt, and then fold into the egg yolk mixture.
3. In a separate bowl, whip the egg whites and cream of tartar until soft peaks form. Gradually add the remaining granulated sugar and continue beating until stiff peaks form. Gently fold the egg whites into the yolk mixture.
4. Spread the batter evenly onto the prepared pan. Bake for 12-15 minutes or until the cake springs back when lightly touched.

5. **Roll the Cake:** While the cake is still hot, carefully roll it up (short end to short end, with the parchment paper still attached). This helps the cake to have a memory of the roll, which will make the final assembly easier. Let it cool completely.
6. **Prepare the Peppermint Whipped Cream:** In a large mixing bowl, beat the heavy whipping cream until soft peaks form. Gradually add the powdered sugar and peppermint extract, and continue beating until stiff peaks form.
7. **Assemble the Roll:** Carefully unroll the cooled cake. Spread a generous layer of peppermint whipped cream over the cake, leaving a small border around the edges. Re-roll the cake without the parchment paper.
8. **Garnish and Serve:** Place the roll on a serving platter, seam side down. Garnish with crushed candy canes or peppermint candies. Slice and serve.

Serving Suggestion: The Chocolate Peppermint Roll is a testament to the wonders of winter flavors. Its striking spiral appearance and the play of chocolate and peppermint on the palate promise to be the highlight of any holiday spread, offering joy and comfort in every slice.

Drizzle individual slices with a chocolate ganache or dust with cocoa powder for an extra touch of chocolate. Pair with a cup of hot cocoa for a heartwarming treat.

Day 13: Fruitcake Cookies

Description and Significance:
Fruitcake Cookies encapsulate the festive spirit of the traditional fruitcake, but in a form that's compact, portable, and immediately satisfying. Gone are the days of long waits for the fruitcake to mature; these cookies bring immediate gratification. Infused with a mixture of candied fruits, nuts, and subtle spices, they encapsulate the mosaic of flavors that the holidays are known for, all in one delightful bite.

Fruitcake Cookies Recipe:
Ingredients:
- 1/2 cup unsalted butter, softened
- 1/2 cup brown sugar, packed
- 1 large egg
- 1 tablespoon brandy or rum (optional)
- 1 teaspoon vanilla extract
- 1 1/2 cups all-purpose flour
- 1/4 teaspoon baking soda
- 1/2 teaspoon ground cinnamon
- 1/4 teaspoon ground nutmeg
- 1/4 teaspoon salt
- 1 cup mixed candied fruit (such as cherries, pineapple, and citrus peel)
- 1/2 cup raisins or currants
- 1/2 cup chopped pecans or walnuts

Instructions:
1. **Cream Butter and Sugar:** In a large bowl, cream together the butter and brown sugar until light and fluffy. Beat in the egg, followed by the brandy or rum (if using), and vanilla extract.
2. **Dry Ingredients:** In a separate bowl, whisk together the flour, baking soda, cinnamon, nutmeg, and salt. Gradually add this to the butter mixture, mixing until just combined.
3. **Add Fruits and Nuts:** Fold in the candied fruit, raisins or currants, and chopped nuts until well distributed.
4. **Shape and Chill:** Using your hands or a spoon, shape the dough into two logs, each about 2 inches in diameter. Wrap each log tightly in plastic wrap and refrigerate for at least 2 hours, or overnight.

5. **Preheat Oven:** When ready to bake, preheat your oven to 375°F (190°C). Line a baking sheet with parchment paper.
6. **Slice and Bake:** Unwrap the chilled dough logs and slice them into 1/4-inch thick rounds. Place the rounds on the prepared baking sheet, leaving about an inch between each cookie. Bake for 8-10 minutes, or until the edges are lightly golden.
7. **Cool and Store:** Allow the cookies to cool on the baking sheet for a few minutes before transferring them to a wire rack to cool completely. Once cooled, store in an airtight container.

Serving Suggestion: Channeling the essence of the iconic holiday dessert, Fruitcake Cookies are a delightful twist on tradition. They are perfect for sharing during festive gatherings or gifting in decorative tins. With each bite, they invoke the magic and nostalgia of the holiday season.

These cookies pair wonderfully with a glass of milk, a cup of tea, or even a glass of dessert wine. For added flair, you can drizzle the cooled cookies with a simple icing or sprinkle them with powdered sugar.

Day 14: Mince Pie Pinwheels

Description and Significance:
The Mince Pie Pinwheels are a delightful reinvention of the beloved mince pie, merging tradition with contemporary tastes. While the classic mince pie has a rich history dating back to medieval times, this version offers a playful spin that's equally celebratory.

Flaky layers of puff pastry envelop a spiced fruit filling, resulting in a treat that's both visually striking and tantalizing to the taste buds. Perfect for festive gatherings or intimate holiday moments, these pinwheels capture the essence of the season in a fresh, bite-sized format.

Mince Pie Pinwheels Recipe:
Ingredients:
- 1 sheet of ready-rolled puff pastry (about 250g)
- 1 cup mincemeat (store-bought or homemade)
- 1 tablespoon orange zest
- 1 egg, beaten (for egg wash)
- Icing sugar, for dusting (optional)
- Ground cinnamon, for sprinkling (optional)

Instructions:
1. **Prepare the Puff Pastry:** Allow the puff pastry to come to room temperature if it's been refrigerated. Unroll it on a lightly floured surface and gently roll it out a bit more to smooth out any creases and increase its size slightly.
2. **Add the Mincemeat:** Spread the mincemeat evenly over the entire surface of the puff pastry, leaving a small border around the edges. Sprinkle the orange zest over the mincemeat.
3. **Roll and Slice:** Carefully roll up the puff pastry, starting from one of the shorter edges, to form a tight log. Slice the log into roughly 1-inch wide rounds.
4. **Preheat Oven:** Preheat your oven to 400°F (200°C). Line a baking sheet with parchment paper.
5. **Place and Brush:** Arrange the pinwheel rounds on the prepared baking sheet, ensuring they are not touching. Brush the tops with the beaten egg to give them a golden sheen when baked.
6. **Bake:** Place the baking sheet in the oven and bake for 15-20 minutes, or until the pinwheels are golden brown and the pastry is cooked through.
7. **Serve:** Allow the pinwheels to cool slightly on a wire rack. Before serving, you can dust them with

icing sugar and a sprinkle of ground cinnamon for an extra touch of festive flair.

Serving Suggestion: The Mince Pie Pinwheels are a delightful ode to the flavors and sentiments of yesteryears, reimagined for the modern palate. They bring together the old and the new, offering a whimsical yet deeply nostalgic treat that's sure to become a holiday favorite.

These pinwheels are best enjoyed warm with a dollop of brandy butter or clotted cream on the side. Pair them with a glass of mulled wine or a cup of spiced tea for a heartwarming holiday treat.

Day 15: Coconut Snowballs

Description and Significance:
Coconut Snowballs, much like their name suggests, are reminiscent of pristine snow globes, untouched and gleaming under a winter sun. These bite-sized treats are an elegant embodiment of the serene beauty of a winter landscape!

The lushness of coconut combined with the delicate sweetness of condensed milk makes for a delectable truffle that not only delights the palate but also stirs the soul with its wintry aesthetics. They are as much a feast for the eyes as they are for the taste buds, making them a standout addition to any festive spread.

Coconut Snowballs Recipe:
Ingredients:
- 3 cups unsweetened shredded coconut
- 1 can (14 ounces) sweetened condensed milk
- 1 teaspoon pure vanilla extract
- A pinch of salt
- 1/2 cup powdered sugar (for rolling)
- Optional: 1/2 cup finely chopped nuts (like almonds or walnuts) for added texture

Instructions:
1. **Prepare the Mixture:** In a large mixing bowl, combine the shredded coconut, sweetened condensed milk, vanilla extract, and a pinch of salt. Mix well until everything is well incorporated. If you're using nuts, fold them in now.
2. **Chill:** Place the mixture in the refrigerator for about an hour or until it's firm enough to handle.
3. **Shape the Snowballs:** Once chilled, take the mixture out of the refrigerator. Using your hands, shape them into small balls, about the size of a walnut.
4. **Roll in Sugar:** Place the powdered sugar in a shallow dish. Roll each coconut ball in the powdered sugar until fully coated, giving it a snowy appearance.
5. **Set and Serve:** Place the snowballs on a tray lined with parchment paper. Let them set for about 30 minutes. They can be stored in an airtight container in the refrigerator for up to a week.

Serving Suggestion: Coconut Snowballs offer a delightful escape into a winter wonderland with each bite. Their ethereal appearance coupled with their rich taste ensures they're not only a favorite among coconut lovers but also among those seeking a touch of magic during the festive season.

Coconut Snowballs are delicious on their own, but for an added touch of luxury, consider serving them with a warm chocolate or caramel sauce for dipping. A cup of hot cocoa or chai tea complements these truffles beautifully, elevating the overall tasting experience.

Day 16: Spiced Apple Galette

Description and Significance:
The Spiced Apple Galette is a heartwarming ode to the simplicity and charm of rustic baking. Evoking memories of family orchard visits and the scent of fresh apples simmering on the stovetop, this open-faced pie is a celebration of autumnal bounty and cozy evenings.

The galette, with its imperfectly folded edges, embodies the idea that beauty lies in imperfection. Each bite is a harmonious blend of tender, spiced apple slices resting on a flaky, buttery crust — a testament to the timeless allure of comfort food during the festive season.

Spiced Apple Galette Recipe:
Ingredients:
For the Crust:
- 1 1/4 cups all-purpose flour
- 1/2 teaspoon salt
- 1 tablespoon granulated sugar
- 8 tablespoons unsalted butter, cold and cubed
- 4-6 tablespoons ice water

For the Filling:
- 3-4 medium-sized apples, peeled, cored, and thinly sliced
- 1/4 cup granulated sugar
- 1 teaspoon ground cinnamon
- 1/4 teaspoon ground nutmeg
- 1/4 teaspoon ground allspice
- 1 tablespoon lemon juice
- 2 tablespoons unsalted butter, small diced
- 1 egg (for egg wash)

Instructions:
1. **Prepare the Crust:** In a large bowl, mix together the flour, salt, and sugar. Cut in the cold butter using a pastry blender or two forks until the mixture resembles coarse crumbs. Gradually add ice water, one tablespoon at a time, mixing until the dough just comes together. Shape the dough into a disc, wrap it in plastic wrap, and refrigerate for at least one hour.
2. **Preheat Oven:** Preheat your oven to 375°F (190°C).
3. **Prepare the Filling:** In a large mixing bowl, combine the thinly sliced apples with sugar, cinnamon, nutmeg, allspice, and lemon juice. Toss until the apples are well-coated.

4. **Assemble the Galette:** Roll out the chilled dough on a lightly floured surface into a roughly 12-inch circle. Transfer it to a baking sheet lined with parchment paper. Place the spiced apple slices in the center of the dough, leaving a 2-inch border around the edges. Dot the apples with the diced butter. Gently fold the edges of the dough over the apples, pleating as needed.
5. **Egg Wash:** Beat the egg and brush it over the folded edges of the galette for a golden finish.
6. **Bake:** Place the galette in the preheated oven and bake for 40-45 minutes, or until the crust is golden and the apples are tender.
7. **Serve:** Allow the galette to cool slightly before serving. It's delightful when paired with vanilla ice cream or whipped cream.

Serving Suggestion: The Spiced Apple Galette captures the essence of the holidays: warmth, togetherness, and the joy of sharing good food. It's a beautiful reminder of simpler times and the pure joy that comes from creating something with love and sharing it with those we cherish.

A scoop of vanilla ice cream or a dollop of whipped cream elevates the galette to a sublime dessert. Drizzle with caramel sauce for an extra touch of indulgence.

Day 17: Almond Joy Macarons

Description and Significance:
The Almond Joy Macarons are a delightful fusion of French confectionery art and the cherished flavors of a classic American candy bar. Evoking nostalgic memories of biting into the sweet combination of coconut, almonds, and chocolate, these macarons breathe new life into a beloved treat.

With delicate and delicious almond shells, rich chocolate ganache, and lush coconut center they harmoniously blend sophistication with childhood glee, making them a uniquely delightful offering for the holiday season!

Almond Joy Macarons Recipe:
Ingredients:
For the Macaron Shells:
- 100g almond flour
- 170g powdered sugar
- 3 large egg whites (room temperature)
- 70g granulated sugar
- Pinch of cream of tartar

For the Coconut Filling:
- 1 cup shredded coconut
- 1/4 cup sweetened condensed milk
- 1/2 teaspoon vanilla extract

For the Chocolate Ganache:
- 100g dark chocolate, chopped
- 50ml heavy cream

Instructions:
1. **Prepare the Macaron Shells:** Sift the almond flour and powdered sugar together into a bowl. In a separate bowl, whisk the egg whites with a pinch of cream of tartar until frothy. Gradually add the granulated sugar, continuing to whisk until stiff peaks form. Gently fold the dry ingredients into the egg whites using a spatula until just combined.
2. **Pipe and Rest:** Transfer the macaron batter to a piping bag fitted with a round tip. Pipe small circles onto a baking sheet lined with parchment paper. Tap the baking sheet on the counter to release any air bubbles. Allow the piped macarons to rest at room temperature for about 30 minutes or until they form a skin on top.
3. **Preheat Oven:** Preheat your oven to 325°F (160°C).

4. **Bake:** Once the macarons have rested, place them in the oven and bake for about 12-15 minutes. Allow them to cool completely on the baking sheet.
5. **Prepare the Coconut Filling:** In a bowl, mix together the shredded coconut, sweetened condensed milk, and vanilla extract until well combined.
6. **Make the Chocolate Ganache:** Heat the heavy cream in a small saucepan until it's just about to boil. Pour it over the chopped dark chocolate and let it sit for a minute before stirring until smooth.
7. **Assemble the Macarons:** Once the macaron shells are cool, match them up by size. Spread a thin layer of chocolate ganache on one shell, then place a small dollop of the coconut filling in the center. Sandwich with another shell, pressing gently.

Serving Suggestion: Marrying the timeless elegance of French macarons with the comfort of an Almond Joy candy bar, these treats are bound to be a hit at any holiday gathering. They're a testament to the magic that happens when tradition meets innovation, offering a mouthful of sweet memories and new beginnings with every bite.

These macarons are best enjoyed with a cup of hot cocoa or a coffee, enhancing the rich flavors of almond, coconut, and chocolate.

Day 18: Cherry Chocolate Biscotti

Description and Significance:
Cherry Chocolate Biscotti are a harmonious blend of classic Italian baking and the festive flavors of cherries and chocolate. These twice-baked cookies are known for their signature crunch, making them the perfect companion for a cup of coffee or a steaming mug of hot cocoa.

The inclusion of dried cherries provides a delightful tartness, contrasting beautifully with the rich, velvety chunks of chocolate. As the days grow colder and nights longer, there's comfort to be found in savoring these cookies while wrapped up in a warm blanket, soaking in the festive ambiance.

Cherry Chocolate Biscotti Recipe:
Ingredients:
- 2 1/4 cups all-purpose flour
- 1 1/2 teaspoons baking powder
- 1/2 teaspoon salt
- 1/2 cup unsalted butter, at room temperature
- 1 cup granulated sugar
- 2 large eggs
- 1 teaspoon pure vanilla extract
- 1 cup dried cherries
- 3/4 cup chocolate chunks or chips

Instructions:
1. **Preheat Oven:** Begin by preheating your oven to 350°F (175°C). Line a baking sheet with parchment paper.
2. **Mix Dry Ingredients:** In a medium-sized bowl, whisk together the flour, baking powder, and salt. Set aside.
3. **Cream Butter and Sugar:** In a larger bowl, beat the butter and sugar together until it's smooth and creamy. This should take about 2-3 minutes.
4. **Add Eggs and Vanilla:** Beat in the eggs, one at a time, ensuring each is well incorporated before adding the next. Stir in the vanilla extract.
5. **Fold in Cherries and Chocolate:** Gently fold in the dried cherries and chocolate chunks, ensuring they're evenly distributed throughout the dough.
6. **Shape and Bake:** Divide the dough in half and shape each into a log that's roughly 9 inches long and 2 inches wide. Place them on the prepared baking sheet, ensuring they're spaced apart. Bake for about 25 minutes or until slightly golden.

7. **Cool and Slice:** Remove the logs from the oven and let them cool on the baking sheet for about 10 minutes. After this, transfer them to a cutting board and, using a sharp knife, slice each log diagonally into 1/2-inch-thick slices.
8. **Second Bake:** Lay the slices back on the baking sheet and return them to the oven for another 10-12 minutes, turning them over halfway, until they're dry and golden.
9. **Cool Completely:** Once done, allow the biscotti to cool fully on a wire rack. This ensures they develop their characteristic crunch.

Serving Suggestion: These biscotti encapsulate the joy of the festive season: the warmth of shared memories, the sweetness of indulgence, and the comfort of tradition. Whether as a gift or a personal treat, they're a delightful way to mark the days leading up to Christmas.

Cherry Chocolate Biscotti are best enjoyed dipped into a hot beverage. Their crisp texture softens slightly, infusing the drink with its rich flavors and absorbing some of its warmth.

Day 19: Panettone Muffins

Description and Significance:
Panettone, the iconic Italian Christmas bread, is transformed into a delightful muffin in this recipe. This reinvention takes the grandeur of this festive favorite and makes it more accessible for everyday enjoyment.

These Panettone Muffins carry the essence of the traditional sweet bread, with an airy texture, fragrant aroma of citrus zest, and bursts of sweetness from candied fruits and raisins. They're a beautiful homage to Italian holiday traditions, encapsulated in a personal-sized treat perfect for sharing or savoring alone with a cup of espresso.

Panettone Muffin Recipe:
Ingredients:
- 2 cups all-purpose flour
- 2 teaspoons baking powder
- 1/2 teaspoon salt
- 1/4 cup unsalted butter, softened
- 3/4 cup granulated sugar
- 2 large eggs
- 1 teaspoon pure vanilla extract
- Zest of 1 lemon
- Zest of 1 orange
- 1/2 cup whole milk
- 1/2 cup candied fruits (e.g., orange, citron, cherries)
- 1/2 cup raisins

Instructions:
1. **Preheat Oven and Prepare Muffin Tins:** Preheat your oven to 375°F (190°C). Line a muffin tin with paper liners.
2. **Mix Dry Ingredients:** In a bowl, sift together the flour, baking powder, and salt. Set aside.
3. **Cream Butter, Sugar, and Zest:** In a large bowl, beat together the butter, sugar, lemon zest, and orange zest until the mixture is light and fluffy.
4. **Add Eggs and Vanilla:** Incorporate the eggs one at a time into the butter mixture, beating well after each addition. Stir in the vanilla extract.
5. **Alternate Dry Ingredients and Milk:** Gradually add the flour mixture in three parts, alternating with the milk. Begin and end with the flour mixture. Mix until just combined.
6. **Fold in Fruits and Raisins:** Gently fold in the candied fruits and raisins, ensuring they're evenly distributed in the batter.

7. **Scoop and Bake:** Using an ice cream scoop or a spoon, fill the muffin tins about 3/4 full with the batter. Bake in the preheated oven for 20-25 minutes, or until a toothpick inserted into the center of a muffin comes out clean.
8. **Cool:** Once baked, remove the muffins from the oven and allow them to cool in the tin for a few minutes before transferring them to a wire rack to cool completely.

Serving Suggestion: Reimagining the beloved Panettone into muffin form captures the spirit of the holidays in a fresh and contemporary way. It offers a nod to the past while embracing the present, ensuring that the flavors and memories of yesteryears continue to be cherished and celebrated.

Panettone Muffins are perfect when enjoyed warm with a pat of butter or a drizzle of honey. Pair them with a strong coffee or a glass of sweet wine, just like the traditional Panettone.

Day 20: Glazed Cranberry Orange Loaf
Description and Significance:
The Glazed Cranberry Orange Loaf is a harmonious marriage of tart and sweet, capturing the essence of winter's vibrant flavors. The bright and zesty notes of the orange beautifully complement the tartness of the cranberries, resulting in a moist loaf cake that radiates festivity.

The sweet orange glaze not only adds an additional layer of flavor but also gives the loaf a glossy finish, making it as visually appealing as it is delicious. Every slice embodies the warmth and joy of the holiday season, making it a must-have addition to any festive spread.

Glazed Cranberry Orange Loaf Recipe:
Ingredients:
For the Loaf:
- 2 cups all-purpose flour
- 1 1/2 teaspoons baking powder
- 1/2 teaspoon baking soda
- 1/2 teaspoon salt
- 1 cup granulated sugar
- Zest of 2 oranges
- 1/2 cup unsalted butter, softened
- 2 large eggs
- 1/2 cup fresh orange juice
- 1/2 cup buttermilk or plain yogurt
- 1 teaspoon vanilla extract
- 1 1/2 cups fresh cranberries, roughly chopped

For the Orange Glaze:
- 1 cup powdered sugar
- 2-3 tablespoons fresh orange juice

Instructions:
1. **Preheat Oven and Prepare Pan:** Preheat your oven to 350°F (175°C). Grease and flour a 9x5-inch loaf pan or line it with parchment paper.
2. **Dry Ingredients:** In a medium bowl, whisk together flour, baking powder, baking soda, and salt. Set aside.
3. **Cream Butter, Sugar, and Orange Zest:** In a large bowl, cream together the butter, sugar, and orange zest until light and fluffy.
4. **Add Eggs:** Beat in the eggs one at a time, ensuring each is well-incorporated.
5. **Incorporate Wet Ingredients:** Stir in the orange juice, buttermilk or yogurt, and vanilla extract until combined.

6. **Combine Wet and Dry Mixtures:** Gradually mix the dry ingredients into the wet mixture, stirring just until blended.
7. **Fold in Cranberries:** Gently fold in the chopped cranberries.
8. **Bake:** Pour the batter into the prepared loaf pan and bake for 55-65 minutes, or until a toothpick inserted into the center comes out clean.
9. **Prepare the Orange Glaze:** While the loaf is baking, whisk together powdered sugar and orange juice in a small bowl until smooth. Adjust the consistency by adding more juice or sugar as needed.
10. **Cool and Glaze:** Once baked, allow the loaf to cool in the pan for about 10 minutes before transferring to a wire rack. While still warm, drizzle the orange glaze over the top.

Serving Suggestion: This loaf is perfect for breakfast or dessert, paired with a cup of tea or coffee. The play of tangy and sweet flavors is a delightful treat for the taste buds.

With its radiant hues of red and orange, the Glazed Cranberry Orange Loaf is like a slice of winter sunshine, promising warmth, comfort, and jubilation with every bite. It's a testament to the simple joys that the festive season brings.

Enjoy this cake while it is warm or after it has fully cooled. Slice the loaf into ½-inch to 1-inch slices and enjoy it with warm tea or coffee.

Day 21: Red Velvet Snowflake Cookies

Description and Significance:
Red Velvet Snowflake Cookies are a festive twist on a beloved classic. Their deep, rich red hue is reminiscent of holiday decorations, warm fires, and cozy gatherings. But it's not just their appearance that captivates; their velvety soft texture and cocoa undertones make them a delight for the senses. Stamped with delicate snowflake patterns and dusted lightly with powdered sugar, these cookies encapsulate the serene beauty of a winter's night! That makes them perfect for any Christmas celebration!

Red Velvet Snowflake Cookies Recipe:
Ingredients:
- 2 1/4 cups all-purpose flour
- 2 tablespoons unsweetened cocoa powder
- 1/2 teaspoon baking powder
- 1/4 teaspoon salt
- 3/4 cup unsalted butter, softened
- 1 cup granulated sugar
- 1 large egg
- 2 teaspoons vanilla extract
- 1 1/2 teaspoons red food coloring
- Powdered sugar, for dusting

Instructions:
1. **Dry Ingredients:** In a medium-sized bowl, whisk together flour, cocoa powder, baking powder, and salt. Set aside.
2. **Cream Butter and Sugar:** In a large bowl, cream the butter and sugar until the mixture is light and fluffy.
3. **Add Egg, Vanilla, and Food Coloring:** Beat in the egg, followed by the vanilla extract and red food coloring, ensuring the mixture is well-combined and uniformly colored.
4. **Mix in Dry Ingredients:** Gradually blend in the dry ingredients, stirring just until incorporated.
5. **Chill Dough:** Shape the cookie dough into a disc, wrap it in plastic wrap, and refrigerate for at least 2 hours, or until firm.
6. **Preheat Oven:** Preheat your oven to 350°F (175°C) and line two baking sheets with parchment paper.
7. **Roll and Stamp:** On a lightly floured surface, roll out the dough to about 1/4-inch thickness. Using a

snowflake-shaped cookie cutter (or any other desired shapes), cut out cookies. If you have a stamping tool, now is the time to stamp a snowflake pattern onto the surface of each cookie.
8. **Bake:** Place the stamped cookies on the prepared baking sheets, leaving an inch of space between each. Bake for 10-12 minutes or until the edges are just beginning to brown.
9. **Cool and Dust:** Allow the cookies to cool on the baking sheets for a few minutes before transferring them to a wire rack to cool completely. Once fully cooled, lightly dust with powdered sugar.

Serving Suggestion: Red Velvet Snowflake Cookies are a melding of tradition and creativity, and they symbolize the magic and wonder of the season. With each bite, you're transported to a world where snowflakes dance in the air and joy fills the heart. It's a taste of Christmas in every bite.

Serve these cookies alongside a mug of hot cocoa or warm milk for a comforting treat. Their festive appearance and delightful flavor make them an instant favorite among both children and adults.

Day 22: Midnight Chocolate Chestnut Torte

Description and Significance:
As Christmas Eve draws to a close and the clock nears midnight, the anticipation of Christmas Day is palpable. The Midnight Chocolate Chestnut Torte captures this magical moment of anticipation, with its deep, velvety chocolate layers encasing a heart of sweet chestnut puree.

The fusion of chocolate's richness with the earthy sweetness of chestnuts evokes memories of wintry nights and festive warmth. As the concluding treat in our Advent calendar of recipes, this torte is the ultimate indulgence, serving as the perfect bridge from Christmas Eve to the joyous day that follows.

Midnight Chocolate Chestnut Torte Recipe:
Ingredients:
For the Chocolate Torte:
- 200g dark chocolate (70% cocoa), chopped
- 200g unsalted butter
- 4 large eggs
- 1 cup granulated sugar
- 1 teaspoon vanilla extract
- 1/2 cup all-purpose flour
- Pinch of salt

For the Chestnut Puree:
- 200g cooked and peeled chestnuts
- 1/2 cup heavy cream
- 1/4 cup granulated sugar
- 1 teaspoon vanilla extract

For the Ganache:
- 100g dark chocolate, chopped
- 1/2 cup heavy cream

Instructions:
1. **Prepare the Chestnut Puree:** In a blender or food processor, combine chestnuts, heavy cream, sugar, and vanilla extract. Blend until smooth. Set aside.
2. **Prepare the Chocolate Torte:** Preheat the oven to 350°F (175°C). Grease and line an 8-inch round cake tin with parchment paper.
3. In a heatproof bowl, melt the chocolate and butter in a pot of simmering water. Once melted and smooth, remove from heat and allow to cool slightly.
4. In a separate bowl, whisk together the eggs, sugar, and vanilla extract until pale and fluffy. Gradually fold in the melted chocolate mixture. Sift in the flour and salt, folding gently until just combined.

5. Pour half of the chocolate batter into the prepared cake tin. Spread the chestnut puree evenly over the batter, leaving a small border around the edges. Pour the remaining chocolate batter over the chestnut layer, smoothing the top.
6. Bake for 35-40 minutes, or until a skewer inserted into the center comes out with just a few moist crumbs. Allow to cool in the tin for 10 minutes before transferring to a wire rack to cool completely.
7. **Prepare the Ganache:** Heat the heavy cream in a small saucepan until it just begins to boil. Pour over the chopped chocolate and let sit for a few minutes. Stir until smooth.
8. Pour the ganache over the cooled torte, using a spatula to spread it evenly over the top and sides.
9. **Chill and Serve:** Refrigerate the torte for at least 2 hours to set the ganache.

Serving Suggestion: The Midnight Chocolate Chestnut Torte is a celebration of textures and flavors that resonate with the spirit of Christmas. Its richness and depth make it the perfect dessert to conclude Christmas Eve, heralding the merriment and festivities of the day to come.

Slice the Midnight Chocolate Chestnut Torte using a sharp knife dipped in hot water. Each slice reveals the creamy chestnut center, offering a delightful contrast to the rich chocolate layers. Serve with a dollop of whipped cream or a scoop of vanilla ice cream for added indulgence.

Day 23: Tiramisu Trifle

Description and Significance:
Tiramisu, which translates to "pick me up" in Italian, is a dessert that truly lives up to its name with its invigorating coffee essence. The Tiramisu Trifle is a contemporary twist on this iconic dish, presenting it in layers that showcase each delightful component.

Each spoonful is a dive through the layers, which delightfully captures the soft sponge soaked in rich coffee, the velvety mascarpone cream, and the bitter touch of cocoa. It's an ode to the Italian classic while making it suitable for large festive gatherings where sharing is at the heart of the celebration.

Tiramisu Trifle Recipe:
Ingredients:

For the Sponge:
- 3 large eggs, separated
- 3/4 cup granulated sugar
- 1 teaspoon vanilla extract
- 3/4 cup all-purpose flour

For the Coffee Soak:
- 1 cup strong brewed coffee, cooled
- 3 tablespoons coffee liqueur (optional)

For the Mascarpone Cream:
- 1 cup mascarpone cheese, at room temperature
- 1/2 cup powdered sugar
- 1 teaspoon vanilla extract
- 1 1/2 cups heavy cream

For Layering:
- Unsweetened cocoa powder, for dusting

Instructions:
1. **Prepare the Sponge:** Preheat your oven to 375°F (190°C). Line a 9x13-inch baking pan with parchment paper.
2. Beat egg yolks with 1/2 cup sugar until thick and pale yellow. Stir in vanilla extract.
3. In a separate bowl, whip egg whites until soft peaks form. Gradually add the remaining 1/4 cup sugar and continue whipping until stiff peaks form.
4. Gently fold the egg yolk mixture into the egg whites. Sift the flour over the mixture and fold in gently.
5. Spread the batter evenly in the prepared pan and bake for 12-15 minutes or until golden brown and springy to the touch. Let cool, then cut into small cubes.

6. **Prepare the Coffee Soak:** Mix the brewed coffee with the coffee liqueur (if using) in a bowl.
7. **Prepare the Mascarpone Cream:** In a large bowl, whisk together mascarpone cheese, powdered sugar, and vanilla extract until smooth. In another bowl, whip the heavy cream until stiff peaks form. Gently fold the whipped cream into the mascarpone mixture.
8. **Assemble the Trifle:** In a large trifle dish or individual glasses, start with a layer of sponge cubes. Drizzle the coffee soak over the sponge, ensuring it's moist but not soggy. Spread a generous layer of mascarpone cream over the sponge. Dust with cocoa powder.
9. Repeat the layers, ending with a dusting of cocoa powder on top.
10. **Chill and Serve:** Refrigerate the trifle for at least 4 hours, preferably overnight, to allow the flavors to meld together.

Serving Suggestion: The Tiramisu Trifle marries elegance with ease, making it an impeccable choice for festive dinners. It not only satiates the sweet tooth but also offers a gentle caffeine kick, making it a fitting dessert to conclude a joyous Christmas meal.

Serve the Tiramisu Trifle chilled. As you scoop out servings, ensure each portion captures all the layers, from the cocoa-dusted top down to the coffee-soaked sponge at the bottom.

Day 24: Traditional Yule Log (Bûche de Noël)

History and Significance:
The Yule Log, or *Bûche de Noël* as it's known in France, is a quintessential Christmas dessert that has deep historical roots. The tradition of the Yule log originates from ancient Celtic celebrations of the winter solstice. Families would select a special log, often from a fruit tree, and burn it during the solstice to cleanse the air of the past year's events and bring luck for the upcoming year. As Christianity spread throughout Europe, the tradition was incorporated into Christmas celebrations.

With the advent of modern heating methods, the actual burning of the Yule log became less common. Instead, in France particularly, the tradition was reimagined in the form of a cake by the 19th century – the *Bûche de Noël*. This delightful dessert is a rolled sponge cake, filled and frosted with buttercream or ganache to resemble a log, and often decorated with marzipan or meringue mushrooms, berries, and sometimes a dusting of powdered sugar to mimic snow.

Yule Log (Bûche de Noël) Recipe:
Ingredients:
For the Sponge Cake:
- 4 large eggs, separated
- 3/4 cup granulated sugar
- 1 teaspoon vanilla extract
- 1/2 cup all-purpose flour
- 1/4 cup unsweetened cocoa powder
- 1/4 teaspoon salt

For the Filling:
- 1 cup heavy cream
- 3 tablespoons powdered sugar
- 1 teaspoon vanilla extract

For the Chocolate Ganache:
- 1 cup heavy cream
- 8 oz dark chocolate, chopped

Instructions:
1. **Prepare the Sponge Cake:** Preheat the oven to 375°F (190°C). Line a 10x15-inch jelly-roll pan with parchment paper.
2. Beat egg yolks with 1/2 cup sugar until thick and pale. Mix in vanilla.
3. In another bowl, whisk together the flour, cocoa powder, and salt. Gradually fold this into the yolk mixture.

4. Beat the egg whites until soft peaks form. Gradually add the remaining 1/4 cup sugar and beat until stiff peaks form. Gently fold this into the batter.
5. Spread the batter evenly in the prepared pan. Bake for 12-15 minutes or until the cake springs back when lightly touched.
6. Once baked, quickly invert the cake onto a clean kitchen towel dusted with powdered sugar. Peel off the parchment paper and roll the cake up in the towel. Let it cool completely.
7. **Prepare the Filling:** Whip the heavy cream with powdered sugar and vanilla until stiff peaks form. Once the cake is cooled, unroll it and spread the filling evenly. Roll the cake back up.
8. **Prepare the Chocolate Ganache:** Heat the heavy cream until it's about to boil. Pour it over the chopped chocolate. Let sit for a minute, then stir until smooth.
9. **Frost the Cake:** Trim the edges of the rolled cake. Cut a small section off from one end at an angle – this will be a "branch" of the log. Position the branch on the side of the main roll using some ganache to adhere. Frost the entire cake with the ganache, leaving the ends exposed. Use a fork to create a bark-like texture on the ganache.

Decoration Tips:
- **Marzipan or Meringue Mushrooms:** These are traditional and add a whimsical touch to the Yule log. For marzipan mushrooms, shape marzipan into stems and caps, attaching them with a bit of chocolate. For meringue mushrooms, pipe meringue into cap and stem shapes, bake until set, then "glue" together with chocolate.

- **Powdered Sugar:** Lightly dusting the log with powdered sugar will resemble fresh snow.
- **Berries and Herbs:** Fresh cranberries, red currants, or sprigs of rosemary can be added for color and to resemble holly.
- **Chocolate Shavings:** These can resemble bark and add an extra layer of texture.

Serving Suggestion: The Yule Log is not just a treat for the palate, but also a celebration of history and the transformation of traditions over time. Its visual appeal and deep-rooted significance make it a perfect centerpiece for the Christmas dessert table.

Slice the *Bûche de Noël* using a serrated knife with a sawing motion to preserve its shape. Allow guests to admire the swirl of the filling, contrasted against the dark chocolate ganache. This cake is rich, so thin slices are often preferred.

Happy baking and enjoy the start of your festive season with these delightful cookies!

Copyright: All rights reserved. No part of this book may be reproduced or transmitted in any form without the written permission of the publisher. Unauthorized use is prohibited and punishable by law.

Printed in Great Britain
by Amazon